Editor-in-Chief
Sharon Coan, M.S. Ed.

Editorial Project Manager
Mara Ellen Guckian

Illustrators
Alexandra Artigas
Kevin Barnes

Cover Artist
Barb Lorseyedi

Art Coordinator
Kevin Barnes

Art Director
CJae Froshay

Imaging
Rosa C. See

Product Manager
Phil Garcia

Publishers
Rachelle Cracchiolo, M.S. Ed.
Mary Dupuy Smith, M.S. Ed.

Author
Angela Krebs, M.S. Ed.

Teacher Created Materials, Inc.
6421 Industry Way
Westminster, CA 92683
www.teachercreated.com
ISBN-0-7439-3255-2
©2002 Teacher Created Materials, Inc.
Made in U.S.A.

The classroom teacher may reproduce copies of materials in this book for classroom use only. The reproduction of any part for an entire school or school system is strictly prohibited. No part of this publication may be transmitted, stored, or recorded in any form without written permission from the publisher.

Table of Contents

Introduction 3
Ways to Use These Books 4
Putting the Books Together 5
Letter to Parents 6
Science Standards 7
Suggested Activities for Science Mini Books 8
    Life Cycles—The Circle of Life 10
    Color Mixing—Crazy Colors 12
    Seeds—Fruits Have Seeds 14
    Plants—Growing Plants 16
    Habitats—Where Do Animals Live? 18
    Five Senses—My Five Senses 20
    Dental Health—My Healthy Smile 22
    Season Cycle—Seasons Change 24
    Matter—What's the Matter? 26
    Food Pyramid—Healthy Me, Healthy You 28
    Food Pyramid 30
Mathematics Standards 31
Suggested Activities for Mathematics Mini Books 32
    Colors—Color My World 34
    Spatial Relationships—Hide and Seek 36
    Addition and Subtraction—I Can Add and Subtract 38
    Recognizing Coins—My Piggy Bank 40
    Patterning—Patterns 42
    Shapes—Shapes 44
    Shapes—Shapes All Around 46
    Sorting and Classifying—Sorting 48
    Three-Dimensional Shapes—The Shape of Things 50
    Telling Time—What Time Is It? 52
    Measurement—Measuring Mania 54
    Measurement Tools 56
Social Studies Standards 57
Suggested Activities for Social Studies Mini Books 58
    Self—All About Me 60
    Hanukkah—Celebrating Hanukkah 62
    Community—Community Helpers 64
    Conservation—Earth Needs You 66
    Safety—Fire Safety 68
    Christmas—Here Comes Christmas! 70
    Emotions—I Have Feelings 72
    Home—My House 74
    Citizenship—Where I Live 76
    Manners—Do You Have Good Manners? 78
    Good Manners 80

Introduction

Fill-In Mini Books was designed to meet the needs of young learners as they embark on the road to literacy. The mini books offer unique and interactive ways for children to become fully involved in the process of reading and writing. Educators are constantly searching for new ways to actively engage students in the learning process. Fostering a positive attitude toward reading can be the single most important thing a teacher is responsible for imparting to his or her students. With a positive attitude, students take pride in their learning and are eager to learn more. They become life-long learners.

Fill-In Mini Books was created to encourage life-long learning. The mini books can be used for content introduction, assessment, or guided reading. The mini books have been proven to be effective as they offer the following:

- predictable text for emergent readers

- wider word spacing to facilitate the mastery of voice-print matching (pointing to each word as it is read) and word segmenting

- cloze activity form to strengthen comprehension and writing skills—students "close" the activity by filling in the blanks

- multiple opportunities for student illustrations

- content-related topics for science, mathematics, and social studies correlated to the K/2 curriculum

Students develop confidence as they collect their books and begin to read them with ease. Rereading the books at home or to classmates continues to strengthen literacy skills while reinforcing the content of each book.

Ways to Use These Books

The mini books included in this book were designed to complement existing units of study. They can be implemented in a variety of ways in the classroom and at home. Some uses are listed below:

Guided Reading Instruction: Correlating literature with the content areas can be an expensive task. To alleviate this problem, *Fill-In Mini Books* provides a simple approach. The books can be reproduced so that each student has a personal copy that can be kept for continued practice. Each book lends itself to literacy skills such as vocabulary, punctuation, capitalization, cloze, and sight vocabulary.

Class Big Books: Each mini-book page can be enlarged to facilitate activities for whole-group instruction. Big books can be used in conjunction with the activities listed at the front of each section to introduce new materials or concepts. Books can then be assembled and placed in the classroom library or reading area for further reading.

Parents as Partners: Use the letter on page 6 of this book to introduce fill-in mini books to family members. Choose a book related to your current unit of study. Construct a book for each child and place it in a baggy. Send it home with each child with directions for completion. The student can complete the book with his or her family and return it to school. He or she can then share the book by reading it to the class or in a small group.

Circle Readings: When books are completed, have students bring them to the circle. Give each child a highlighter. Reread the book together as the students voice-print match. Ask students to locate certain sight words or punctuation marks. When located, encourage the students to highlight them. When the books go home, the highlighted words serve as a clear indication of what needs to be practiced.

Storing the Books

As an introductory activity, have children make a special "Book Box" using a shoe box, a pizza box, or similar container. (Shoe stores and pizza restaurants are often willing to donate boxes for classrooms.) The box can be saved to collect and store the mini books at home or at school as completed. Creating the special storage containers will help demonstrate the importance of their books and their reading.

Putting the Books Together

Fill-In Mini Books was designed to be student friendly. Thick black lines are provided to aid in the cutting process. Each page is numbered for easy ordering of the pages during assembly. Space is provided on each mini page for students to illustrate the concepts they are learning. Write-on lines offer adequate space for students to fill in their ideas as the various topics are explored. Each book can be assembled in the manner listed below.

Step 1
Copy the two-page mini book for every student.

Step 2
Instruct the children to cut along the thick black lines on each page. Assist with proper hand position for cutting.

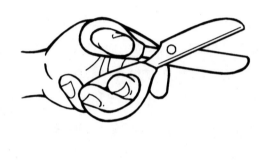

Step 3
Put the cover to the side and assist children in ordering the pages 1–7. (**Note:** Provide numeral cards to assist with number recognition at the beginning of kindergarten.)

Step 4
Demonstrate how to place the cover on top of the stack of pages and staple the book together. If necessary, have an adult assist with the stapling procedure.

Date:_____

Dear Parent(s),

During the course of the year, your child will be reading and creating many types of books. Among them will be fill-in mini books that your child will complete and illustrate. We will be using these mini books to enrich our content-area curriculum and to reinforce many literacy skills.

Please help your child create a special place to keep these books for future reference and reading. This can be accomplished by decorating a bag or box and using it to store the mini books. You might want to label it with your child's name and make a point of explaining its use to other family members.

Please encourage your child to reread these mini books to you as well as other members of his/her family. As he or she reads, please take the time to ask questions and praise him or her for a job well done. You will be amazed to see your child become a confident young reader and writer.

If you have any questions, please feel free to contact me.

Sincerely,

_____

Teacher

Science Standards

The students will be able to observe and identify patterns of daily, monthly, and seasonal changes in their environment.
The Circle of Life   Seasons Change

The students will be able to observe and identify weather conditions.
Seasons Change

The students will be able to describe how plants and animals depend on each other and the non-living environment.
Fruits Have Seeds   Growing Plants
Where Do Animals Live?

The students will be able to identify the states of matter and representations of each.
What's the Matter?

The students will describe the factors that help promote good oral health.
My Healthy Smile

The students will describe the factors that help promote a healthy body and describe elements of the Food Pyramid as a means to achieve this.
Healthy Me, Healthy You

The students will name the five senses and the body part associated with each.
My Five Senses

The students will explore the primary color wheel and the creation of new colors when two are combined.
Crazy Colors

©Teacher Created Materials, Inc.   7   #3255 Fill-In Mini Books

Suggested Activities for Science Mini Books

The activities below are offered to introduce or supplement each mini-book presentation. Some mini books will be simpler than others to introduce as the concepts are familiar to the students. The ideas below should serve to explain or expand upon questions that might arise with each new topic.

The Circle of Life

A great way to observe the circle of life is to raise caterpillars. Check related websites, science catalogs, or your local conservation office to find out how to acquire them. Provide your students with photographs or drawings of each stage of the life cycle. It is important to use proper vocabulary such as *pupa* and *chrysalis* when discussing this process. Butterflies make a *chrysalis,* while moths make *cocoons*.

Crazy Colors

A great way to mix colors for this activity is to use watercolors. However, color mixing can also be accomplished by using colored pencils or crayons. Be sure to model the activity so the children color the appropriate free-form shape completely and accurately. Another great way to explore color mixing is by using food coloring and eye droppers. Have the students drip food coloring onto a coffee filter with an eyedropper. The colors will be absorbed in the filter and run together. Another option is to use straws to release colored water onto a piece of paper. Have students blow through the straw to mix the colors.

Fruits Have Seeds

The wonders of living things are amazing to young children. They will be intrigued by the notion of eating seeds, roots, and stems. Provide many types of seeds. They can be used for counting, comparing, graphing, and sorting. For this book activity, have apples, oranges, pumpkins, pears, and a watermelon available for the children to dissect and to investigate the seeds. Each child can glue a sample of the seeds on to the appropriate pages.

Growing Plants

Often, young children do not perceive plants as living things. Provide the children with many varieties of plants from greens to flowering plants. Planting flowers from a seed in a clear cup is a great way to observe plant growth. The clear cup allows for observation of root growth. Another great way is to grow seeds in a clear baggie with a moist paper towel. Keep the bag sealed and it will act as a portable terrarium. The bags can be attached to the classroom windows. Cups can be placed on the window sill or on trays and taken outside each day.

Where Do Animals Live?

Provide many literature resources for the different habitats: ocean, forest, pond, zoo, farm, jungle, rain forest, or river. Ask parents to participate in a "Family Project" by doing the following: Each student will select a habitat. They will build the habitat inside of a box (diorama). Included with the project should be a written piece that names the habitat, where it can be found in the world, and two animals that live there. The students bring the projects to class and share them with their friends.

Suggested Activities for Science Mini Books (cont.)

My Five Senses

Exploring the five senses lends itself to many multi-sensory activities. For *sight*, have the children work in pairs with one student blindfolded. Have the sighted child give oral directions to his or her partner to draw various shapes or simple pictures. For *smell*, place balls of cotton in baby food jars. Moisten the cotton balls with various scented items. Cover the jars with cheesecloth or netting and tie with ribbon. Have the students smell each jar to determine the scent. For *touch*, make a "Mystery Box" or "Feely Box" and place an object inside. Have a student feel the object in the box, describe it orally, and give clues. Classmates can guess what the object is. For *hearing*, have students close their eyes while a student makes noises, plays instrument, runs water, or makes other audible sounds. For *taste*, have students compare sour, bitter, salty, and sweet foods. Discuss the different areas of the tongue that are sensitive to each type of taste.

My Healthy Smile

Have many visuals available that depict tooth structure and care. Invite a dentist or a hygienist to your classroom. He or she can illustrate proper brushing techniques and healthy dental habits. Students can practice flossing using strips of upside-down egg cartons and yarn. A great way to show the function of teeth is to use instruments and items such as a nutcracker (crushing), knife (cutting), and a fruit roll-up (tearing).

Seasons Change

Have students make a chart of appropriate weather patterns for each season. A nice visual might be the wheel on page 1 of the mini book. Children can see that the seasons have a particular order regardless of temperature or weather. A paper plate can be divided into four quadrants and labeled for each season. Leaves, seed pods, snowflakes, flowers, etc., can be added to suggest the appropriate season.

What's the Matter?

Science experiments are a great hands-on approach that will be meaningful for students. For solids, liquids, and gases do the following: Place ice cubes (*solid*) in a small pan. Place the pan on a hot plate or stove. Observe the ice melting to water (*liquid*). Let the water boil so that evaporation takes place and steam is observed (*gas*). Have the students record their observations in a science journal.

Healthy Me, Healthy You

Providing information that will lead to a health-conscious child is very important. When children become aware of the purpose for eating healthy foods, they become more likely to try new foods. Provide a graphic organizer of the six sections of the Food Pyramid. Have the children cut out magazine pictures of different foods and and then place the foods in the correct section of the pyramid. A great culminating activity is to have a "Food Pyramid Feast." Have children bring in foods that will illustrate each section of the pyramid and have a potluck luncheon.

Life Cycles

The Circle of Life

By _____

A caterpillar lays its eggs on a _____.

1

The caterpillar _____ the leaf until it is big and fat.

2

The caterpillar gets tired and needs to rest. It makes a _____.

3

Life Cycles

**The caterpillar is
_____.
What will happen next?**

4

**Wow! Look and see. Now it is a beautiful
_____.**

5

**The butterfly will grow up and lay
_____.**

6

Draw the life cycle of a butterfly.

7

Color Mixing

CRAZY COLORS

By _____

Red and yellow make _____.

1

Blue and yellow make _____.

2

Blue and red make _____.

3

Color Mixing

Red and white make

_____.

4

Black and white make

_____.

5

My favorite color is

_____.

6

Color the rectangles to match the color word.

Red

Orange

Green

Yellow

Pink

Gray

Purple

7

Seeds

Fruits Have Seeds

By _____

All fruits have _____.

1

These are _____ seeds.

2

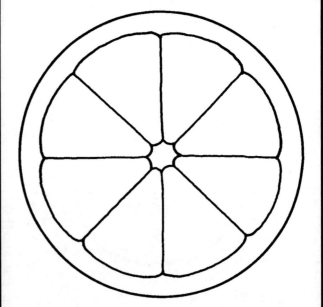

These are _____ seeds.

3

Plants

Growing Plants

By _____

Plants are _____ **things.**

1

They need _____ **to root in.**

2

They need the

_____

to make food and keep their leaves green.

3

Plants

They need _____ to drink.

4

A plant needs _____ just like we do.

5

Plants do not like _____.

6

Draw 3 things that a plant needs.

7

Habitats

Where Do Animals Live?

By _____

This is a forest.

_____ and

_____

live in a forest.

1

This is an ocean.

_____ and

_____

live in an ocean.

2

This is a pond.

_____ and

_____

live in a pond.

3

Habitats

This is a jungle.

_____ and
_____

live in a jungle.

4

This is a farm.

_____ and
_____

live on a farm.

5

This is a zoo.

_____ and
_____

live at a zoo.

6

This is me. I live in a
_____.

7

Five Senses

My Five Senses

By _____

I can see with my
_____.

I can see
_____.

1

I can hear with my
_____.

I can hear
_____.

2

I can smell with my
_____.

I can smell
_____.

3

Five Senses

I can taste with my
_____.
I can taste
_____.

4

I can feel with my
_____.
I can feel
_____.

5

This is me. I have
_____ senses.

6

Draw a picture to show which body part you use for each sense.

See   **Hear**

Taste   **Smell**

Feel

7

Dental Health

My Healthy Smile

By _____

I have a healthy

_____.

1

I brush my teeth

_____ a day.

2

I _____

my teeth too.

3

Dental Health

I visit the _____ twice a year.

5

I eat healthy _____ and drink lots of _____.

6

All of these things will help keep my _____ shiny and bright.

7

Label the parts of a tooth. Use these words:

root

enamel

pulp

8

Season Cycle

Seasons Change

By _____

There are _____ seasons.

1

This is _____.
I am _____.

2

This is _____.
I am _____ leaves.

3

Season Cycle

This is _____.

People shovel

_____.

4

This is _____.

I am planting a

_____.

5

_____

is my favorite season.

6

Use the space below to tell about something you do during your favorite season:

_____
_____
_____
_____
_____
_____
_____

7

Matter

What's the Matter?

By _____

Matter can be a solid.

_____

is a solid.

1

Solids can be many

_____.

2

Matter can be a liquid.

_____

is a liquid.

3

Matter

Liquids are the shape of their _____.

4

Matter can be a gas.
_____ is a gas.

5

Gases are _____.
We can not see them.

6

Matching Matter

Water

Oxygen

Wood

Metal

Juice

Helium

Solid

Liquid

Gas

7

Food Pyramid

Healthy Me, Healthy You

By _____

A _____
is a fruit.
Fruits are healthy foods.

1

_____
is a vegetable.
Vegetables are healthy foods.

2

_____
is a dairy product.
Dairy products are healthy foods.

3

Food Pyramid

A _____
is a protein. Proteins are healthy foods.

4

A _____
is a grain. Grains are healthy foods.

5

_____
are sweets. Sweets are not healthy foods!

6

To be healthy, eat the Food Pyramid way.

7

Food Pyramid

Mathematics Standards

The students will locate and identify colors.
Color My World

The students will classify items with one attribute: color, shape, or size.
Sorting

The students will identify, describe, and extend simple color, shape, and number patterns.
Patterns

The students will develop and demonstrate knowledge of spatial relationships and position.
Hide and Seek

The students will locate and identify two- and three-dimensional shapes.
*Shapes   Shapes All Around
The Shape of Things*

The students will develop the concept of time by identifying intervals to the hour.
What Time Is It?

The students will recognize and name the value of the penny, nickel, dime, and quarter.
My Piggy Bank

The students will manipulate and explore various measurement tools: ruler, scale, thermometer, and pan balance and their purposes.
Measuring Mania

The students will develop and use strategies for addition and subtraction using manipulatives and/or a physical model.
I Can Add and Subtract

Suggested Activities for Math Mini Books

The activities below are offered to introduce or supplement each math-related mini book. Some mini books will be simpler than others to introduce. The ideas below should serve to explain or expand upon questions that might arise with each new topic.

Color My World

Investigating rainbows and using a prism and light are great ways to explore color. Display many labeled examples of the colors you wish to explore. Use food coloring to change the color of various foods such as eggs, frosting, cookie batter, and drinks. Have students sort colored items.

Hide and Seek

Position students around the room and ask other students to verbalize their positions. For example: "Tiara is behind Emily." When students become more comfortable with spatial relationships, have them close their eyes while you place an object in the room. They then can verbalize its position when they locate it. They can also play "I Spy" and the leader can give positional clues.

I Can Add and Subtract

Young children typically view addition and subtraction as a "grown-up" activity and therefore are very eager to learn this concept. It is important for children to learn the key words that tell them when to add (how many in all) and when to subtract (how many are left). This is a great stepping-stone to creating great problem solvers.

My Piggy Bank

Learning the difference between coins can be a difficult task. To minimize frustration, play a variety of games and activities that compare the different coins. For example, provide each student with a template that illustrates circles. Have the students use a magnifying glass to investigate a particular coin. Then have them each draw what they observe on the templates. In the mini book on pages 40–41, students are invited to do rubbings of different coins to illustrate them. To accomplish this, direct students to place the appropriate coin under the mini-book page and rub over the paper with a crayon, creating the image of the coins.

Students love "The Money Game." To play, seat the children in a large circle and give each one a penny. Have the children take turns tossing the penny toward the plate in hopes of getting it in. When all the students have tossed their pennies, discuss how much money is in the plate. If applicable, discuss if trades can be made (5 pennies for a nickel). Continue playing, counting the money in the plate at the end of each round, and making appropriate trades.

Patterns

Repetition is an effective method of teaching patterns. Incorporate the monthly calendar into a patterning excercise. Use a variety of colored shapes. Determine a pattern for each month, beginning the year with a very simple ABAB (red square, blue triangle, red square, blue triangle) type and expanding to more complex patterns as the year progresses. Every morning during calendar activities, have the students identify the next color and shape to be added to the calendar.

Suggested Activities for Math Mini Books (cont.)

Shapes

Identifying shapes can be a difficult skill for young children to master. The difference between a square and rectangle are particularly confusing. These activities can help a great deal: "Stretch a Shape" is a very interactive approach to learning shapes. To play, sew together 4 yards of 1/4" or 1/2" elastic. Discuss with students the characteristics of a particular shape. A triangle for example has three sides so you will need three people. The three students get inside the elastic ring and place it on their backs or ankles. They move backward and stretch the elastic into the needed shape. Continue this activity to create different shapes. Can you make a square from a triangle? What will you need? You will need another person since a triangle has three sides and a square has four sides. Once a square has been made, discuss how to form a rectangle. You don't need more people but you do need to change the length of two sides. Another option is to give each child a rubber band to try the activity using their fingers.

Shapes All Around

Provide many concrete objects for the children to examine. Books, containers, blocks, sports equipment, school tools, etc., can all demonstrate different shape properties. Have the students look closely at the objects and make a pictorial list of all the shapes that can be seen within the object. For instance, a soccer ball is round, but the pattern on it has hexagons. A glue bottle is a rectangle or a cylinder with a triangle on top.

Sorting

Gather small objects that are great for sorting—bottle tops, colored paperclips, marbles, unifix cubes, beans, seeds, buttons, or shells. Collect egg cartons and muffin tins to use as sorting trays. Hula-hoops can be used as sorting rings and can be overlapped to create Venn diagrams. Use large circles of yarn to create giant Venn diagrams in which students can stand. Try sorting those students wearing shoes with laces and those wearing slip-on shoes, or those with long-sleeved shirts and those with short-sleeved shirts.

The Shape of Things

Send a note home for parents to send in boxes and cans of various sizes and shapes. Make a floor graph to compare three-dimensional shapes of the objects brought to school. Obtain a set of solid three-dimentional shapes. Let the children explore each shape to see which shapes slide, roll, or slide and roll. Have them make an observation record.

What Time Is It?

Learning the order of numerals and the purpose of the minute and hour hands are essential components in understanding time. To offer a hands-on approach, try "The Human Clock." Make numeral cards 1–12 and laminate them for durability. Place them clockwise in a large circle on the floor. Have students take turns using their bodies to create the hour hand and the minute hand to show the given time. When they become more proficient, make large hands out of oaktag that the students can move.

Measuring Mania

Have many measuring tools available including a scale, ruler, a yardstick, a tape measure, measuring cups, measuring spoons, a pan balance, and a thermometer. Let the children explore each measurement tool and its purpose. Discuss why we use different tools for different jobs.

Colors

Color My World

By _____

I see red.

_____

are red.

1

I see orange.

_____

are orange.

2

I see yellow.

_____

are yellow.

3

Colors

I see green.
_____
are green.

I see blue.
_____
are blue.

I see purple.
_____
are purple.

How many colors do you see?

Spatial Relationships

Hide and Seek

By _____

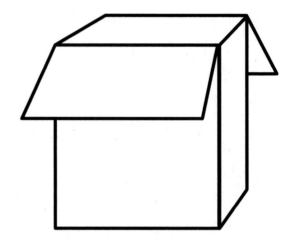

The dog is **inside** the box.

1

I am **outside** the house.

2

The ball is **on** the seal's nose.

3

Spatial Relationships

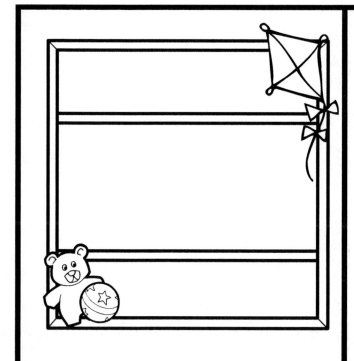

A toy is on the <u>middle</u> shelf.

4

A bird is on <u>top</u> of the tree.

5

A child is <u>between</u> the trees.

6

I am _____

_____

_____.

7

Addition and Subtraction

I Can Add and Subtract

By _____

Mommy bought 3 apples. I ate one. Now there are _____ apples.

1

I had 3 pieces of candy. My sister gave me 2 more. Now I have _____ pieces of candy.

2

I had 6 pennies. I lost 2 of them. Now I have _____ pennies.

3

Addition and Subtraction

6 birds were sitting in a nest. 3 flew away. Now there are _____ birds in the nest.

4

2 friends were playing at the park. 1 friend came to join them. Now there are _____ friends at the park.

5

When I add, I put things _____.
When I subtract, I take things _____.

6

Write a math story for this picture.

_____
_____
_____

7

Recognizing Coins

My Piggy Bank

By _____

My piggy bank has a

_____.

1

Make heads and tails rubbings of a penny in this space.

A penny is worth

_____.

2

My piggy bank has a

_____.

3

Recognizing Coins

Make heads and tails rubbings of a nickel in this space.

A nickel is worth

_____.

4

My piggy bank has a

_____.

5

Make heads and tails rubbings of a dime in this space.

A dime is worth

_____.

6

This piggy bank has a quarter. A quarter is worth

_____.

7

©Teacher Created Materials, Inc. 41 #3255 Fill-In Mini Books

Patterning

Patterns

By _____

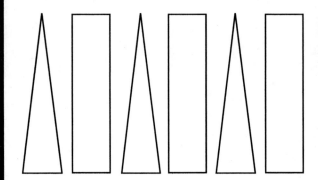

This is a _____ pattern.

1

Can you make a shape pattern?

2

▢○○▢○○▢○○

1　2　1　2　1　2

This is a _____ pattern.

3

#3255 Fill-In Mini Books	42	©Teacher Created Materials, Inc.

Patterning

Can you make a number pattern?

4

There are _____ patterns too.

5

Can you make a color pattern?

6

What kind of pattern is this?

This is a _____ pattern.

Make your own pattern.

7

Shapes

Shapes

By _____

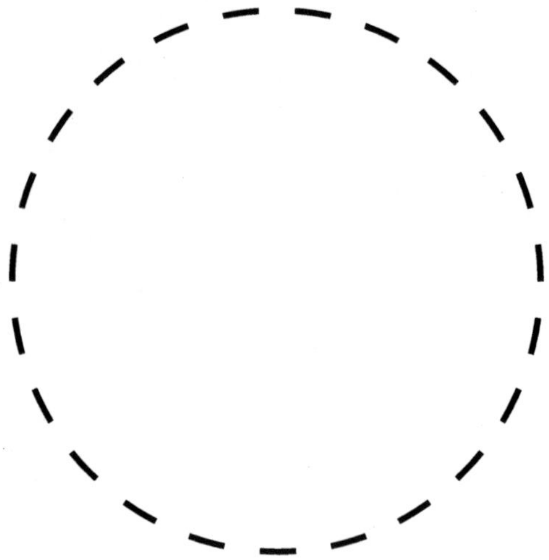

This is a circle.

1

This is a square.

2

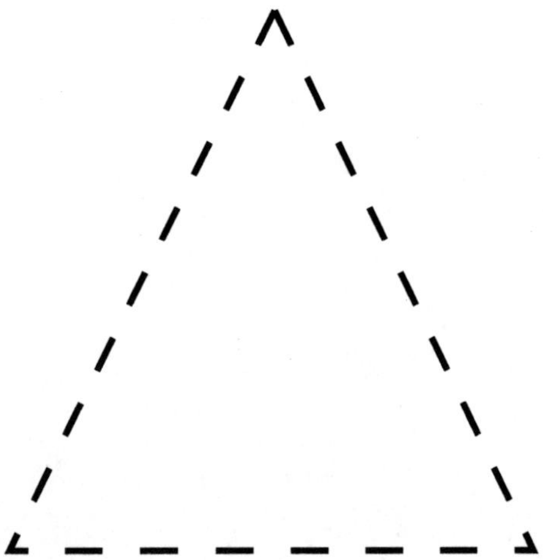

This is a triangle.

3

#3255 Fill-In Mini Books — 44 — ©Teacher Created Materials, Inc.

Shapes

This is a rectangle.

4

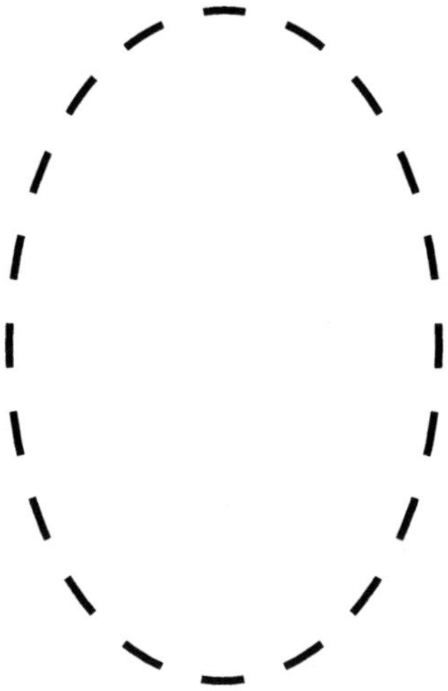

This is an oval.

5

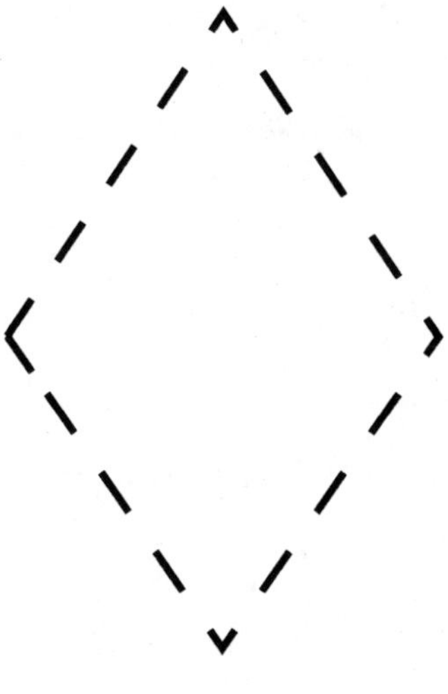

This is a diamond.

6

Draw a picture using these shapes.

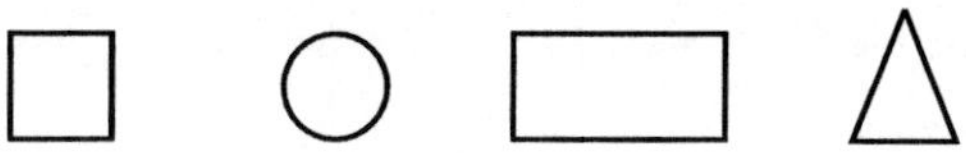

□ ○ ▭ △

7

Shapes

Shapes All Around

By _____

This is a present. I can see a _____.

1

This is a bicycle. I can see three_____.

2

This is a train. I can see a _____.

3

Shapes

This is an ice-cream cone. I can see a _____.

4

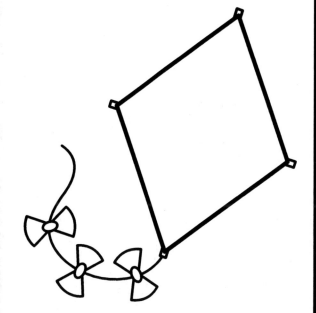

This is a kite. I can see a _____.

5

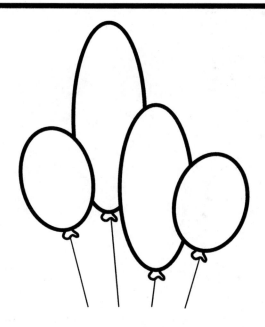

These are balloons. I can see _____.

6

Shapes are all around!

7

Sorting and Classifying

Sorting

By _____

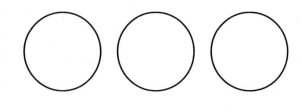

These circles are sorted by

_____.

1

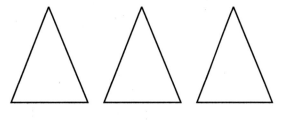

These shapes are sorted by

_____.

2

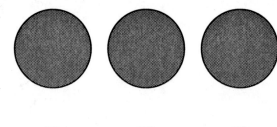

These circles are sorted by

_____.

3

Sorting and Classifying

I can sort by size!

4

I can sort by shape!

5

Draw 2 groups showing sorting by color.

Draw 2 groups showing sorting by size.

I can sort by color!

6

7

Three-Dimensional Shapes

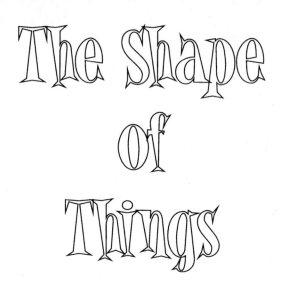

Exploring 3-Dimensional Shapes

By _____

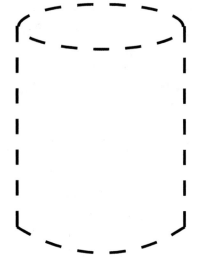

I can make a cylinder.

A can is a
_____.

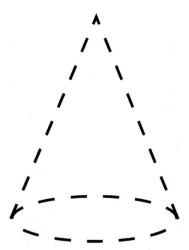

I can make a cone.

Three-Dimensional Shapes

A birthday hat is a
_____.

4

I can make a cube.

5

A present can be a
_____.

6

Name these 3-dimensional shapes.

_____

_____

_____

7

©Teacher Created Materials, Inc.   #3255 Fill-In Mini Books

Telling Time

What Time Is It?

By _____

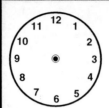

It is _____.

It is time to wake up.

1

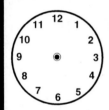

It is _____.

It is time to go to school.

2

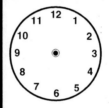

It is _____.

It is time for lunch.

3

Telling Time

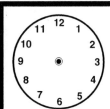

It is _____.
It is time to go home.

4

It is _____.
It is time for dinner.

5

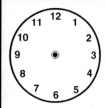

It is _____.
It is time to read a story.

6

It is _____.
It is time to go to bed.
Goodnight!

7

Measurement

Measuring Mania

By _____

A thermometer measures

_____.

It is _____ degrees.

1

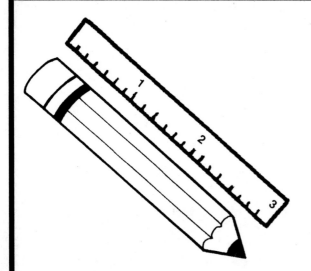

A ruler measures

_____.

The pencil is _____ long.

2

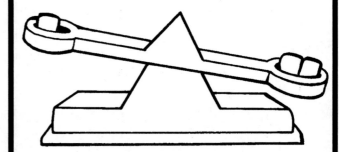

A pan balance will tell if

something is _____

or _____.

3

Measurement Tools

A scale measures _____.

4

I weigh _____ pounds.

5

I would like to measure _____.

I will use a _____.

6

Name these objects used for measuring things.

_____

_____

_____

7

Measurement Tools

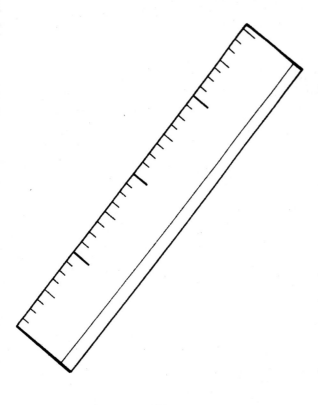

ruler

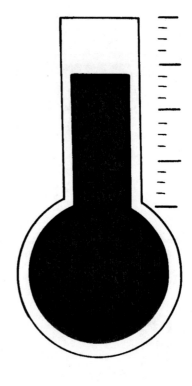

thermometer

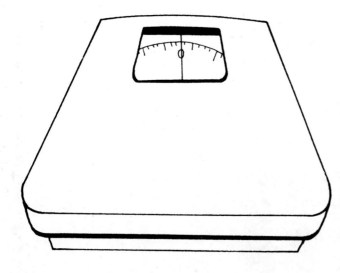

scale

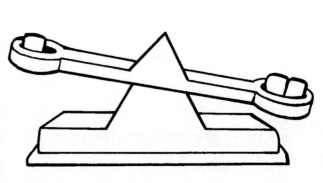

pan balance

Social Studies Standards

The students will use pictures and maps to locate community places.
Where I Live

The students will be able to identify ways in which humans have altered the environment and the effects of those changes.
Earth Needs You

The students will be introduced to cultural celebrations as a means to foster cultural diversity and tolerance. The students will recognize different traditions and customs.
Celebrating Hanukkah   Here Comes Christmas!

The students will recognize the uniqueness of self and others.
All About Me

The students will recognize and name community helpers that are present in their community.
Community Helpers

The students will name ways to prevent fires and develop a family safety plan.
Fire Safety

The students will observe and practice good manners as a means to communicate effectively with others.
Do You Have Good Manners?

The students will name the basic feelings: happy, sad, scared, mad, surprised, and glad and articulate situations asscociated with each.
I Have Feelings

The students will describe their dwellings in terms of purpose and need.
My House

Suggested Activities for Social Studies Mini Books

The activities below are offered to introduce or supplement each social studies mini book. Some mini books will be simpler than others to introduce. The ideas below should serve to explain or expand upon questions that might arise with each new topic.

All About Me

Learning personal information, such as an address or telephone number, promotes personal safety in young children. An awareness of self as a unique individual allows children to accept differences among people. After completing this mini book, students can make a class graph of favorite colors, eye or hair color, or favorite sports.

Celebrating Hanukkah

It is important to make children aware of cultural diversity, and to foster acceptance of others. To explore the Jewish tradition of Hanukkah, read stories to your students that explain the miracle of the oil and the purpose of the celebration, or have a student who celebrates the holiday share his or her family traditions. Purchase a wooden dreidel and teach the children how to play the dreidel game. Use gold foil-covered coins or counters for gelt in the game. Making latkes and applesauce is another great Hanukkah activity. Many math lessons can be incorporated into cooking activities. Check your favorite website for recipes.

Community Helpers

Community helpers play an important role in the lives of young children. Many are seen as heroes or a representation of occupations children aspire to have as adults. Invite as many community helpers to visit your students as possible. Ask the guests to wear their uniforms, if applicable, and discuss their jobs with the students. Fire and police stations are also great places to visit and often offer special programs for young students. Provide dress-up clothes for various occupations (doctor, nurse, dentist, business person, fireman, policeman, teacher, mailman) so the children can dramatize the role of each helper.

Earth Needs You

Earth Day is celebrated on April 22. Have your students work in cooperative pairs to create Earth Day posters with appropriate slogans. The posters can be distributed to local businesses for display or hung around the school. The students can also participate in a "Family Project" which promotes recycling. Have families collect plastic and glass bottles. The students can keep a record of the amount of plastic or glass they recycled by keeping a recycling log. The money earned from deposit returns can be saved to buy flowers or a sapling to be planted around the school at the conclusion of the school year.

Suggested Activities for Social Studies Mini Books (cont.)

Fire Safety

Send home a piece of graph paper with each student and have your students work with their parents to create a safety plan. The plan should include two escape routes out of the home as well as a safe place to meet away from their homes. Have students mark where smoke detectors are found in their homes. Most communities have fire safety programs and firefighters will willingly come to your classroom to promote fire safety.

Here Comes Christmas!

Teaching children the spirit of "giving" and not "getting" at this time of year can be a difficult task. Instead of focusing on what they would like to receive for Christmas, focus on what they can give their community for Christmas. Local food pantries would cherish grocery bags decorated with holiday themes. The bags can be used when giving holiday meals to the needy. Check with your local grocery store about donating brown grocery bags. Local nursing homes will welcome holiday cards decorated by young children and hospitals will distribute small crafts made by the children to those who cannot go home for the holiday.

I Have Feelings

Learning how to verbalize feelings is difficult for some young children. However, learning to identify feelings is an important step in understanding their behaviors, needs, and wants. To illustrate various emotions, have posters available that illustrate each feeling. You can also have a "Clown Day" and invite volunteers to help you design the students' faces with clown faces. The students then act out the type of clown face they are wearing.

My House

Provide a large dollhouse with furniture, figures, and accessories for your class. Work together to furnish the house, room by room. While doing so, discuss why certain items are in particular rooms. Also discuss the purpose of various items such as beds, tables, chairs, and a bathtub. Share books and pictures of different types of homes.

Where I Live

Young children are very egocentric. They believe the world exists for them and them alone. Learning that they are a part of a larger community is very interesting for them. Provide them with many visuals. Begin with pictures of homes and streets. Talk about the neighboring area. Expand to include postcards, pictures of local landmarks, and travel brochures of the area, if appropriate. Discuss the state and the country in which you live. Later, introduce items, such as maps appropriate for your area, and a globe.

Do You Have Good Manners?

Dramatization and role-playing are effective ways to practice the use of manners. At the conclusion of the unit, a great way to test-drive those manners is to have a dining experience at a local diner or pizza parlor. If this is not possible, set up a restaurant in the classroom. Use page 80 to create a list of rules important to your students. Post the list in the classroom and share it with parents.

Self

All About Me

By _____

My name is _____.

I am _____
years old.

1

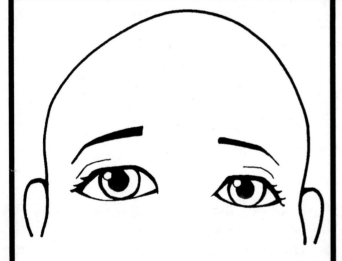

I have _____
hair and_____
eyes.

2

My address is

_____

_____

_____.

3

#3255 Fill-In Mini Books ©Teacher Created Materials, Inc.

Self

My favorite color is
_____.

4

I like to play with my friend,
_____.

5

We like to play_____
_____.

6

When I grow up I want to be a _____.

7

Hanukkah

Celebrating Hanukkah

By _____

Hanukkah celebrates the miracle of the _____.

1

The oil lasted for _____ days.

2

The_____ has eight candles.

3

Hanukkah

**Families make potato
_____ to eat.**

4

**Children spin the
_____.**

5

Hanukkah is a special celebration for families.

6

Draw a symbol of Hanukkah and label it.

7

Community

Community Helpers

By _____

Many _____ work in our community.

1

A _____ puts out fires and teaches us how to be safe.

2

A _____ protects us and makes sure people follow rules.

3

Community

A _____
delivers mail to our house.

4

A _____
helps to keep us healthy and makes us feel better when we are sick.

5

A _____
helps our family teach us how to read and write.

6

Draw a picture of another community helper below.

This is a _____.

7

Conservation

Earth Needs You

By _____

Earth needs your

_____.

Here's what you can do.

1

Always put your garbage in a _____.

Keep Earth clean!

2

Turn the water

_____

while you brush your teeth.

Save water!

3

#3255 Fill-In Mini Books © Teacher Created Materials, Inc.

Conservation

When you leave a room, turn the _____ off. Save electricity!

4

Plant a _____ or some _____. Help make Earth pretty.

5

Recycle _____ and _____.

6

Be kind to Earth. It's the only one we have!

7

Safety

Fire Safety

By _____

Never play with _____.

1

Stay away from hot things like _____ and _____.

2

If you see a fire, never go near it. Find a safe place to call _____.

3

Safety

If you see smoke, stay low and _____. Never hide!

4

If your clothes catch on fire, _____, _____, and _____.

5

Make sure your house has working smoke _____ on every floor.

6

Make a safety _____ with your family.

7

Christmas

Here Comes Christmas!

By _____

Snow is _____.

1

We decorate a special Christmas _____.

2

We wrap _____.

3

Christmas

We send Christmas
_____
to our friends and family.

4

We hang our
_____
out on Christmas Eve.

5

It is Christmas Day! We
_____
with family and friends.

6

Write about your favorite part of Christmas.

_____
_____
_____
_____
_____
_____
_____
_____
_____
_____

7

Emotions

I Have Feelings

By _____

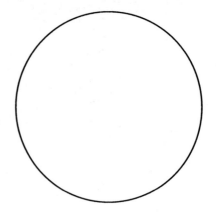

Sometimes I'm happy.
I was happy when
_____
_____.

1

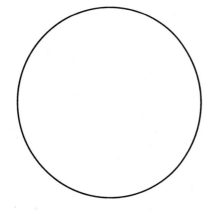

Sometimes I'm sad.
I feel sad when
_____
_____.

2

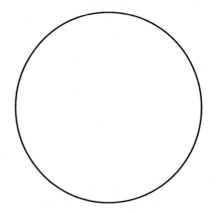

Sometimes I'm scared.
I feel scared when
_____
_____.

3

Emotions

Sometimes I'm <u>mad</u>.
I was mad when

_____

_____.

4

Sometimes I'm <u>surprised</u>.
I was surprised when

_____

_____.

5

Sometimes I'm <u>glad</u>.
I feel glad when

_____

_____.

6

I like when I feel

_____!

7

©Teacher Createed Materials, Inc.

Home

My House

By _____

My house has _____ rooms.

1

I sleep in my _____.

2

I eat breakfast, lunch, and dinner in the _____.

3

Home

I watch television in the
_____.

4

I take a bath and brush my teeth in the
_____.

5

This is a picture of my house.

6

This is a picture of the people who live at my house.

7

Citizenship

Where I Live

By _____

My home is in

_____.

1

My neighborhood is part of

a _____.

2

I live in the city of

_____.

3

Citizenship

My city is part of a

_____.

4

I live in the state of

_____.

5

My state is part of a

_____.

6

The country I live in is

_____.

I love my country!

7

Manners

Do You Have Good Manners?

By _____

Do you say "_____
_____"
when someone is in your way?

1

Do you say "_____
_____"
when you ask for something?

2

Do you say "_____
_____"
when someone gives you something?

3

Manners

Do you wait your _____ when you are in line or playing a game?

4

Do you _____ your toys with friends?

5

Do you clean up your _____ when you are finished playing?

6

Well! I guess you do have good manners. You should be proud of yourself.

7

Good Manners

1. _____

2. _____

3. _____

4. _____

5. _____